BEATING FRAUD IS EVERYONE'S BUSINESS: securing the future

Presented to Parliament by
the Secretary of State for Social Security
by Command of Her Majesty,
July 1998

SOCIAL SECURITY 50 YEARS
CELEBRATING THE PAST
LOOKING TO THE FUTURE

Cm 4012

£8.65

Contents

Foreword

from the Prime Minister

This Government is committed to a radical reform of the welfare state. The system was created 50 years ago, when society was very different. So much has changed since: job mobility instead of the 'job for life', more women going out to work, more people having occupational pensions and other savings, and the increase in single-parent families. The welfare state must change too.

We need a modern welfare system, which meets today's needs. We have set out to build it, based on the principles of work for those who can, and security for those who cannot. Earlier this year we produced a clear statement of our aims and principles in *New ambitions for our country: A NEW CONTRACT FOR WELFARE*. This also included a commitment to a programme of individual reforms, starting with the child support reforms published earlier this month, and set out targets so that everyone can see the progress we are making.

We made the task of tackling fraud one of our early priorities. This is because public support is vital for welfare reform, and public support is eroded by the failure to stop people defrauding the benefit system.

We are also taking a new approach to cracking down on fraud. Previous governments had made some advances in detecting fraud once it had been committed. We will build on this. But we need to go further. Our strategy includes two radical new approaches.

First, we will minimise the opportunity to commit fraud in the first place by improving the administration of the benefit system. When the chance comes up, we will also redesign benefits themselves to make them far more difficult to abuse.

Second, we will work across boundaries – with all Government departments, and with local authorities and others – to share expertise and create a professional approach to anti-fraud work. We will work in partnership with banks, insurance companies and others who have experience of large-scale, organised fraud to keep one step ahead of the criminals.

All kinds of fraud, from petty 'fiddles' through to criminal gangs setting out to defraud the system of hundreds of thousands of pounds, take money away from where it is needed most. We have a duty to stop it being syphoned off by fraudsters so that we can improve services for those genuinely in need.

The sheer size and complexity of the social security system makes this a real challenge. We must make sure that those in need do not lose out and we must deal effectively with hundreds of thousands of transactions every day quickly and accurately. Designing fraud out of the system, and working together to beat the criminals, will help us achieve this.

This Green Paper sets out what we have achieved in the last year and the steps we are taking this year and beyond. It also asks for your views on the best way of tackling fraud. Public support for our anti-fraud initiatives is vital. That is why we are publishing this consultative paper, and why we will report every year on the progress we have made.

Prime Minister

Summary

Introduction

1 The Government is committed to creating a modern welfare state which meets the needs of society today. The new welfare contract which the Government is building with the nation, gives equal weight to ensuring:

- **a first class modern service which responds to individual beneficiary's needs; with**
- **those who are eligible, claiming and receiving their entitlement; and with**
- **benefits going only to those who are entitled to them.**

2 Such a system relies crucially on public confidence that the money they contribute is spent wisely and securely. However, that public confidence cannot be sustained if fraud pervades the system.

3 Social security fraud is a threefold evil:

- **it is stealing billions of pounds from the public;**
- **it takes money which could otherwise be spent on those genuinely in need; and**
- **it strikes at the roots of public support of our welfare system.**

4 That is why a strategy to counter fraud is central to the Government's agenda for welfare reform.

Vision

5 Our vision is continuous improvement:

- **to minimise fraud in the social security system, so as**
- **to maximise the resources available to meet need, and**
- **to enhance public confidence.**

The level of fraud

6 We will never know exactly how much fraud there is in social security. By its nature, fraud is concealed. On a conservative estimate, fraud steals some £2 billion a year from the total programme spend of £100 billion.

- **That £2 billion could be used to meet the cost of Income Support for the one million pensioners who do not currently take up their entitlement *and* to pay £2 a week extra in Child Benefit for 12 million children.**

7 The sums at stake could be very much larger, around £7 billion a year if suspicion of fraud is included.

- **£7 billion would cover the cost of Income Support take up for the one million pensioners *plus* paying every pensioner a £10 bonus each week.**

8 Details of these estimates, and an account of the weaknesses in the current systems are in Chapter Two.

9 Fraud occurs in many ways. The public assumes that most fraud is low value, for example the individual working while claiming, or a mother claiming as a lone parent but living with a partner. Even these frauds, which start out relatively small, can end up costing far more.

- **One woman stole nearly £60,000 by fraudulently continuing to claim a pension after her mother's death.**

10 The public is less aware of fraud by landlords and employers.

- **A landlord received £2,500 Housing Benefit each week for 50 'tenants' in properties controlled by him; only 10 of these tenants were actually resident, he created 20 fictitious identities, 20 tenants left some time ago and were replaced by new tenants not on benefit but the landlord carried on collecting Housing Benefit: a fraudulent income for the landlord of £100,000 a year.**
- **An employer paid her 20 employees £3.60 an hour, but gave them time off to sign on as unemployed; her honest competitor was paying £4.60 an hour: a fraudulent increase in the first employer's profits which cost the taxpayer £40,000 a year.**

11 On top of all this, there are a number of far more sophisticated frauds, by organised criminals, where the sums are much larger.

- **One highly organised group of criminals dishonestly obtained benefit order books in London, and then skilfully altered the details so the books could be cashed in other parts of the country. Losses are estimated to be in excess of £14 million.**
- **Another organised gang was detected making numerous fraudulent claims based on false identities at 600 addresses using forged and manipulated Portuguese identity cards. Losses to taxpayers amounted to over £2 million.**

12 These organised frauds are much more difficult to detect, and would seldom be identified in the surveys which estimate the overall level of fraud. This is one reason why the £2 billion estimate above is conservative: we cannot with any confidence estimate the extent of very sophisticated fraud.

Aims

13 The Government's strategy for tackling fraud, and achieving its vision, is guided by four aims (see Chapter Three). The aims themselves, and the action planned, have been set on the basis of the Government's assessment of the weaknesses in the social security system.

Aim One

To develop an anti-fraud culture among staff and the public and to deter fraud.

Aim Two

To design and operate policies and systems which minimise fraud.

Aim Three

To create an environment in which the work against fraud can flourish.

Aim Four

To develop a highly-skilled anti-fraud profession.

■ Aim One

To develop an anti-fraud culture among staff and the public and to deter fraud.

14 The **problem** is that while more than 90 per cent of people see organised fraud as wrong in all circumstances, only one in five people see low value individual fraud as serious, and only half would see themselves having any responsibility to assist the Government fight fraud. Indeed, less than half believe the Government is really committed to punishing fraudsters, yet over 90 per cent would welcome greater punishment for systematic organised fraud.

Our strategy is:

- **to demonstrate we mean business in countering systematic organised fraud, and to present a comprehensive picture of the types and amounts of all types of fraud to win public support for tackling the lost opportunities for public spending across the board.**

■ Aim Two

To design and operate policies and systems which minimise fraud.

15 This will involve improvements in five areas: benefit design, individual case management, detection, environment, and evaluation.

Benefit design

16 The **problem** is that existing benefit rules and business systems are allowing too much fraud to occur in the first place.

Our strategy is:

- **to review the benefit rules, in particular those that are most frequently broken, to ensure they reflect the right balance between costs, the level of fraud and, critically, public support for action against fraud;**
- **to promote security considerations in any development of new policy; and**
- **to review funding arrangements so that prevention is rewarded alongside detection (see also Aim Three).**

Individual case management

17 The **problem** is that welfare services have often been passive, rather than actively helping people move towards work and independence, and with an emphasis on paying out money promptly rather than focusing on accuracy. A number of prototypes of the Government's Active Modern service are already operating.

Our strategy is:

- **to build on the prototypes, and implement improved business processes across the whole social security system, using risk management techniques to target activity effectively;**
- **to improve the level of staff compliance with these processes; and**
- **to collect, store and provide staff with access to social security data in a way which reduces duplication and error, and increases our ability to prevent fraud.**

Detection

18 The **problem** is that however good we become at preventing fraud, most identified fraud occurs as people's circumstances change, after an initial claim. So detection and constant vigilance remains essential.

Our strategy is:

- **to increase the risk of detection through better use of technology;**
- **to identify inconsistencies in customer information across different benefit systems, and with other agencies (such as Inland Revenue);**
- **to improve the targeting of checks like home visits and other techniques of active case management; and**
- **to spread experience among investigators through improved professionalism (see also Aim Four).**

Enforcement

19 The **problem** is that very few fraudsters are ever effectively penalised for their action. Over the last few years an average of only 12,000 cases were prosecuted, and 35 per cent of successful prosecutions in Magistrates' Court lead only to conditional discharge. Practice among local authorities is mixed: some have never prosecuted anyone for Housing Benefit fraud.

Our strategy is:

- **to make punishment a reality for proven fraudsters;**
- **to make maximum use of the newly introduced administrative penalties and cautions;**
- **to bring more cases to court, where penalties are greater (for example, under the Theft Act);**
- **to prosecute some small-scale frauds, so that there are no 'safe' frauds immune from prosecution; and**
- **to establish greater consistency in the treatment of fraud across different agencies (and reviewing the financial incentives to do so).**

Aim Three

To create an environment in which the work against fraud can flourish.

20 We need improved systems for **funding and performance measurement.** The **problem** is that, while the previous Government invested in activities specifically related to countering fraud, there was less emphasis on incentives and resources for front-line processing. Fraud investment was established on the basis that agencies achieve benefit savings from **finding** fraud, rather than **preventing** fraud occurring. In the search for these savings, different agencies were effectively encouraged to compete, rather than work co-operatively, against fraudsters.

Our strategy is:

- **to develop more robust approaches to performance measurement, including local measures of the level of fraud;**
- **to assess investment against these improved criteria for success; and so**
- **to incentivise proactive work wherever it can deliver reductions in fraud.**

Securing greater co-operation

21 The **problem** is that our approach to fraud is often parochial, with insufficient co-ordination and co-operation across Department of Social Security and local authority benefit administration, with other central government and public bodies (whose paperwork, for example, helps define identity), or with institutions facing fraud in the private sector (for example, insurance and credit card companies) especially from organised gangs.

Our strategy is:

- **to be inclusive, involving all the stakeholders in design and implementation, both practitioners and policy makers. This will involve new ways of working.**

Aim Four

To develop a highly-skilled anti-fraud profession.

22 The **problem** is that a lack of common training across Benefits Agency and local authorities has led to some fraudsters being dealt with less effectively than others; and that, in the absence of standards for skills, of good practice, and a code of conduct, anti-fraud officers do not always apply their skills in a consistent and fair way.

Our strategy is:

- **to establish anti-fraud work on a professional basis, with professional training and accreditation, principles of good practice and conduct moving, as these practices are put in place, towards a highly professional body of anti-fraud staff.**

23 Further details of the Government's approach in each of these areas are set out in Chapters Four to Seven. A timetable of action is in Chapter Eight. The Government's view of the system in 2020 is in Chapter Nine.

Conclusion

24 This Green Paper sets out the overall strategy for tackling fraud. With this framework set, the task is not only to implement the wide range of initiatives already identified, but also to be vigilant in identifying further action, monitoring the changing patterns of fraud in order to frustrate new attacks.

25 The Government is committed to making a difference on fraud, as a key element of its plan to create a modern welfare state, in which the people can have confidence.

26 We have the responsibility to put things right This Green Paper sets out the Government's strategy. We would welcome your views.

27 Please write to the following address:

The Fraud Green Paper Consultation Team
Department of Social Security
6th Floor
The Adelphi
1-11 John Adam Street
London WC2N 6HT

You can also respond by using the following email address:

counterfraud@ade004.dss.gov.uk

Comments should reach us by 30 September 1998.

Responses will normally be available to the general public unless you specifically ask us to keep your views confidential.

Chapter One

Introduction

1.1 Our commitment to reform the welfare state is central to the Government's plans for the modernisation of Britain, in this Parliament and beyond. Crucial to our success will be public support. To maintain that support we must be able to show that the system is secure, with money only going to those who are entitled to it.

1.2 While stamping out fraud is therefore central to our welfare reform aims, it is only one of a number of objectives to which the Government gives equal importance.

1.3 The new welfare contract which the Government is building with the nation gives equal weight to ensuring:

- **a first class modern service which responds to individual beneficiary's needs;**
- **that those who are eligible, claim and receive their entitlement; and**
- **that benefits go only to those who are entitled to them.**

1.4 In this new welfare contract, the Government's duty is to design a secure system and deliver an Active Modern Service. In return, it is the citizen's duty not to defraud the system.

1.5 This Green Paper sets out the Government's strategy for tackling fraud, taking forward the seventh principle in our Green Paper: *New ambitions for our country: A NEW CONTRACT FOR WELFARE,* that:

- **the system should encourage openness and honesty and the gateways to benefits should be clear and enforceable.**

1.6 The Green Paper covers:

- **how much fraud there is now and the weaknesses in the present system which make social security fraud so easy (Chapter Two);**
- **our strategy for the future, built around four aims which address the current weaknesses (Chapter Three);**
- **our plans for delivering each aim (Chapters Four to Seven);**
- **a timetable of action (Chapter Eight); and**
- **our vision for social security in 2020 (Chapter Nine).**

Chapter Two

Where are we now?

2.1 With expenditure of £100 billion a year, social security is by far the largest single Government budget. The great majority of our customers are honest. But we are a large organisation dealing with money and information and, in common with similar institutions such as banks and insurance companies, we are a target for organised and opportunistic fraud and abuse.

2.2 Internal Department of Social Security reviews confirm that our budget is under attack from two quite different directions:

- **from a large number of individuals, finding ways to commit fraud among the plethora of detailed rules governing the benefits; and**
- **from organised attempts at major fraud each involving enormous sums of public money.**

2.3 The system's complexity also means that we are vulnerable to mistakes leading to incorrect payments, even where there is no intention to defraud. For example, with 33 million changes of circumstances reported each year to the Benefits Agency alone, there is substantial scope for error. Claimants do not always fully understand when to report a change, what to report, or whether a call to one agency notifies all the others that might also be involved. The collection and assessment of millions of pieces of information over many years has also produced a system where the data is not always reliable and includes fraudulent identities.

The level of social security fraud and incorrect payments

2.4 Measuring the level of fraud in the system is difficult. By its nature, fraud is concealed. But, since we have personal details for everyone in receipt of benefit, it is possible to investigate samples of claims in detail to try and establish levels of fraud. Starting only as recently as 1994, the Department of Social Security has run a series of reviews of fraud and incorrectness in individual benefits – the *Benefit Reviews*. Beginning with Income Support and continuing with eight other benefits including Housing Benefit, Disability Living Allowance and Retirement Pension, these reviews have so far covered some 84 per cent of annual benefit expenditure.

2.5 Building on this preliminary work, the Government intends to overhaul how fraud is calculated. On the current basis the headline findings of these studies are as follows (definitions are explained in the Annex):

- **by value, 93 per cent of benefit payments are correct;**
- **some 2 per cent of payments by value are fraudulent;**
- **there is strong suspicion of fraud on a further 3 per cent;**
- **there is low suspicion of fraud on 2 per cent; and**
- **a small fraction of a per cent, which nonetheless amounts to around £150 million in net terms, is being overpaid annually as a result of incorrectness, though this is a balance between overpayments of £750 million (roughly equally due to the Department of Social Security and customers respectively) and underpayments of £600 million (around three-quarters due to customers).**

2.6 Applying these findings to the annual programme spend of £100 billion:

- **a conservative estimate of fraud is *£2 billion* a year; but**
- **the figure could be much higher, around *£7 billion* if all suspicions of fraud were well founded.**

2.7 Fraud at £2 billion a year is equivalent, for example, to paying the unclaimed Income Support to Britain's poorest one million pensioners **and** £2 a week extra on Child Benefit to 12 million children. £7 billion fraud is the equivalent of paying each pensioner an additional £10 a week as well as ensuring that Britain's poorest million pensioners claim their full Income Support entitlement.

2.8 More fraud could probably be discovered by use of more intrusive checks on the claimants chosen randomly for the *Benefit Reviews*. But that would raise issues of public acceptability, given that there is no prior assumption that the claim is fraudulent.

2.9 The results of the reviews are, therefore, not only subject to margins of sampling error, but also the uncertainty that even more in-depth investigation might potentially uncover more sophisticated fraud. Nevertheless, the reviews are the best available information.

2.10 The reviews have helped identify the main frauds relating to different benefits. For example, the main fraud uncovered on review of Unemployment Benefit was working while still claiming benefit. The main frauds on Housing Benefit were in relation to earnings and benefit claimed for addresses where claimants are not actually living. For Invalid Care Allowance the main frauds were failure to care and having earnings above the allowed limit. Further analyses are included in the Annex.

2.11 Examples of how concealed frauds can come to light occur regularly as part of the investigation of organised fraud. What begins as an apparently minor anomaly, or single instance of benefit fraud, can eventually turn out to be one small element of a very much larger organised fraud, sometimes stretching beyond social security (for example, into mortgage fraud). Two such cases are summarised below:

- **suspicion over a single Housing Benefit claim led to observations being carried out at the address. The investigation led to three people taking part in multiple claim fraud in excess of £250,000;**
- **suspicions by Post Office staff over the number of change of address forms that had been requested, which later led to GIRO cheques being presented with false addresses. The investigation found nine people were involved and the fraud was in excess of £130,000.**

2.12 Having illustrated the broad scale of fraud in the system, the next section identifies the most important weaknesses in our current approach to security.

Weaknesses in the current system

2.13 The previous administration made a start in tackling fraud, towards the end of its years in office, and focusing largely on detecting low value fraud. Staff across Department of Social Security agencies and local authority benefit administration put substantial effort into this programme to catch fraud.

2.14 But there was no comprehensive strategy, and there are weaknesses in five key areas.

2.15 First, public **attitudes** to fraud are equivocal: cases of greed are condemned, but some small scale fraud is almost condoned as relieving need (even though most citizens manage on state benefits without recourse to fraud). Not all the rules which we try to police command public confidence in all quarters. For example, the single/living together distinction in the benefit system sits uneasily with the complexity of many people's lives.

2.16 Second, our systems are not sufficiently secure to **prevent** fraud from occurring in the first place, because of:

- **patchy information on what fraud is occurring where, and how;**
- **little attention to security issues in both policy design and operational delivery – too often fraud work is an afterthought;**
- **patchy application of controls on the procedures for benefit processing, exacerbated by conflicting requirements for accuracy and speed of processing; and**
- **little financial incentive to invest in prevention rather than detection.**

2.17 Third, while the ability to **detect** fraud once it has occurred improved considerably under the previous Government, there remain weaknesses because:

- **there is still limited use of data across different systems to identify suspicious cases;**
- **the current financial incentives promote competition between different agencies, rather than co-operation; and**
- **the specialist investigative staff, in particular in local authorities, operate without the mutual support, external recognition, and the opportunities to share expertise that would be provided in any other profession.**

2.18 Fourth, the procedures to **sanction** fraudsters at the lower end of fraud have up to now been largely ineffective. In recent years an average of only 12,000 cases were taken to court by the Department of Social Security, and 35 per cent of successful prosecutions in a Magistrates' Court ended in a conditional discharge. In many local authorities there are no prosecutions at all for Housing Benefit fraud. The low numbers of sanctions, and the inconsistency of approach across the social security system, significantly undermines the deterrence not to commit fraud.

2.19 Fifth, the approach to fraud is too **parochial**, with insufficient co-ordination

- **across Department of Social Security agencies and local authorities involved in front line benefit delivery, where local agreements have not been as effective as they should be;**
- **across other parts of central government (for example, with Departments responsible for documents such as birth certificates or passports, or proof of immigration status); and**
- **with the private sector, especially where organised fraud is concerned.**

2.20 We will not make substantial inroads into fraud by continuing with piecemeal initiatives. We need a major change in gear. This requires a clear statement of strategy, and the political commitment to deliver on fraud, working in partnership with others across the public and private sectors.

Conclusion

2.21 There is clear evidence that very substantial sums are being paid incorrectly, both in genuine error but also because of fraud. The systems for delivering social security, and the environment in which they operate, do not produce the level of security necessary for a modern service.

2.22 To change this, the Government is committed to a systematic, across the board, assault on fraud and incorrectness. Our strategy is set out in the following chapters.

Chapter Three

Our strategy

3.1 The Government is committed to creating a modern welfare state which meets the needs of society today.

3.2 Such a system relies crucially on public confidence that the money they contribute is spent wisely and securely (and most citizens on state benefits manage without recourse to fraud). However, that confidence cannot be sustained if fraud pervades the system.

3.3 Fraud in social security is a threefold evil:

- **it is stealing;**
- **it takes money which could otherwise be spent on those genuinely in need; and**
- **it strikes at the roots of public support of our welfare system.**

3.4 This is why the Government has made it a priority for welfare reform to crack down on fraud. Our new welfare contract spells out the duties of Government and the duties of citizens. One key element of this new contract is the duty of the Government to devise a system that is transparent and open, and gets money to those in need. And the reciprocal duty of the citizen is not to defraud the taxpayer.

Vision

3.5 It is important also that positive consequences of tackling fraud are kept clearly in sight. So our vision is continuous improvement:

- **to minimise fraud in the social security system, so as**
- **to maximise the resources available to meet need, and**
- **to enhance public confidence.**

3.6 The Government has set out four aims, to give direction to detailed measures to deliver this vision.

Aim One

To develop an anti-fraud culture among staff and the public and to deter fraud.

Aim Two

To design and operate policies and systems which minimise fraud.

Aim Three

To create an environment in which the work against fraud can flourish.

Aim Four

To develop a highly-skilled anti-fraud profession.

Each aim is described in turn below.

Aim One

To develop an anti-fraud culture among staff and the public and to deter fraud.

3.7 Everyone has a responsibility in the fight against fraud.

3.8 Public attitudes can be a significant deterrent to anti-social behaviour, whether defrauding the social security system or, for example, drinking and driving. There is, though, no common attitude across all types of fraud, with small scale fraud almost condoned in some minds, despite the large total cost and the impact on public confidence. The Government is intent on enlisting support for our strategy by presenting an accurate picture of the types, scale and significance of fraud and by ensuring that small scale fraud is avoided through efficient operation of the social security system.

3.9 Those claiming benefits must understand their duty to back claims with evidence, and report changes in their circumstances. Staff delivering benefits and working with National Insurance accounts must understand the central place for accuracy and security.

3.10 The role of education, to influence attitudes and deter fraud, is therefore key to the success of the strategy.

Aim Two

To design and operate policies and systems which minimise fraud.

3.11 Because we deliver social security through a very large and complex system, fraud can occur in many ways. We are committed to improvement through delivery of our Active Modern Service. We must seize the opportunity to build security into our redesigned systems from beginning to end: from the design of policy through to the delivery and policing of benefit payments. We must leave behind the world where anti-fraud work is synonymous only with reactive detection and investigation. We need a comprehensive strategy across the whole spectrum of prevention, detection and enforcement.

Aim Three

To create an environment in which the work against fraud can flourish.

3.12 We need to work against fraud in an environment that itself encourages and enables that effort. We must ensure that the funding of social security administration, and the financial incentives in the system, favour prevention and do not simply reward detection. In turn, we must build greater co-ordination across local and central government, and across the public and private sectors, for a sustained drive against fraud. We will need the help and co-operation in particular of local authorities and the Audit Commission, working alongside the Benefit Fraud Inspectorate.

Aim Four

To develop a highly-skilled anti-fraud profession.

3.13 Current images of staff who tackle fraud are misleading. Fraud has for too long been seen as unimportant, and work to tackle it has been seen as obtrusive, or even draconian. The need for expert staff to tackle fraud has not been considered a priority. Yet in drawing up an effective strategy for anti-fraud work, we must deal with highly professional, educated fraud entrepreneurs as well as less sophisticated, lower value benefit fraud.

3.14 The following four chapters set out how we will achieve each of these aims.

Chapter Four

Culture

Aim One

To develop an anti-fraud culture among staff and the public and to deter fraud.

Public attitudes

4.1 Research into public awareness of social security fraud, and attitudes towards it, has been conducted since the last election.

4.2 This research[1] shows that **three-quarters of people think that, in general, social security fraud is a crime, and that two-thirds view it as no different from stealing.**

4.3 Most of the public's direct experience is likely to be of small-scale fraud by benefit claimants. Publicity around serious organised fraud cases in the courts has led to an awareness also of organised attacks on the system (often carried out by people from abroad), but there is generally much less awareness of systematic fraud involving employers or landlords.

4.4 People tend to differentiate between serious organised fraud and lower level benefit fraud by claimants. While nearly everyone (94 per cent) considers that systematic and organised fraud is wrong in all circumstances, **there is a degree of sympathy for people living on benefits who supplement their income by occasional earnings which they then fail to declare as they should.** Only one person in five currently feels that this type of fraud is a serious matter, with some people indicating that they could easily imagine how they might do such things themselves. Such **fraud can even be seen as a legitimate activity,** with only half of the people surveyed saying that they would report it.

4.5 Yet such fraud 'costs' other people in need dearly. The estimate of fraud in just Income Support and Jobseeker's Allowance – £450 million – is equal to paying over 10 million pensioners £3.50 extra per month, or adding 70 pence to the weekly rate of Child Benefit for 12 million children.

4.6 There is also evidence to suggest that **the public would welcome greater punishments for people who commit social security fraud** than they believe currently occur. Nearly everyone (over 90 per cent) thinks that systematic abuse should be dealt with either by imprisonment or by a fine or repayment order.

[1] Counter Fraud Publicity Evaluation: Research Surveys of Great Britain for the Central Office of Information – Feb 1998; Counter Fraud Publicity Development: Andrew Irving Associates for the Central Office of Information – Nov 1997; Counter Fraud Publicity: Navigator for the Central Office of Information – April 1998.

4.7 The challenge is therefore to demonstrate that we mean business when we say **we will tackle organised fraud.** In order to win over public support for the Government in its strategy of reducing all types of fraud, we also need to present a more comprehensive picture of the nature and amounts of all types of fraud, and to explain the public expenditure opportunities which are lost due to high volume, low value fraud.

Presentation of anti-fraud work

4.8 The most effective **deterrent** for those who would commit fraud which will always be **peer group disapproval and pressure.**

4.9 Alongside welfare reforms designed to have positive and lasting effects on the lives of people by **encouraging positive behaviour,** the communication of our work and objectives can **deter negative behaviour** such as involvement in social security fraud, and tolerance towards it.

4.10 **We are not going to change attitudes overnight.** The experience of 30 years of anti-drink/driving campaigning suggests that self-regulating behaviour in respect of social security fraud is likely to be a long-term goal. We will need to continually repeat and reinforce our evolving message and to ensure that we get, and retain, full support from all sections of society and from across the political spectrum.

4.11 Our strategy for changing attitudes includes effective presentation, linking fraud and welfare reform messages, to enhance public confidence in the system by:

- **making a real connection between savings from fraud work and improvements to service delivery, to meet public concern that money saved from anti-fraud work should be returned to the taxpayer;**
- **continuing to dispel the notion that fraud is a victimless crime;**
- **consistently presenting action on more serious, complex fraud as well as lower level benefit fraud;**
- **publicising tough action against people who continue to commit fraud;**
- **changing perceptions of the work of fraud investigators, to get away from the image of the snooper; and**
- **explaining the positive benefits of new techniques, such as data-matching and the safeguards which exist in relation to their use.**

4.12 The Government will develop a public communication strategy around these themes.

Staff culture

4.13 As well as affecting public attitudes, it is also important to develop a strong security culture among the **staff** administering benefits. Many current staff are only too aware of fraud, and want to deliver a quality service which is properly secure. We must build on this, and promote understanding of what we are trying to achieve. We must ensure that staff understand the importance of adhering to security requirements, in order to underpin the changes in systems and processes which are described in the next section.

4.14 We also need a system which acknowledges secure working practices and deals with insecure practices: **a culture of compliance with the security rules and procedures** that we create. While developing better policies, techniques and training, we must also require managers and staff to operate systems correctly. In order to draw on the ideas of staff for improving performance against fraud, we need regular and structured feedback from frontline staff to managers.

4.15 The security culture and attitudes of staff, even those not directly employed in investigative work, can be positively affected by:

- **underlining the importance of security in job descriptions and work objectives;**
- **the weight given to security in performance appraisal and performance pay processes; and**
- **provision of better fraud awareness and training.**

4.16 We must also promote understanding of, and commitment to, our strategy by **other departments and organisations** whose work can impact on our security. While fraud has risen up the political agenda in recent years, we must do more to ensure that our plans for tackling fraud receive appropriate **support and resources**.

Other factors influencing culture

4.17 Progress in other areas covered by this report will also play a major part in bringing about an anti-fraud culture, for example by:

- **providing an efficient service to claimants and one where security is clearly a priority. A good example is the service we are developing for single mothers which simplifies their initial claim to benefit, but also allows us to maximise compliance with child support rules with staff trained to recognise and refer incidents of potential fraud to the Benefits Agency;**
- **devising effective staff targets and incentives. An example here is the new performance indicators which we are testing with staff in Yorkshire, focusing on the quality of investigations rather than simply measures of detection; and**

- **developing the professionalism of staff engaged on fraud and security work. A joint team of Benefits Agency and local authority fraud investigators has just finalised an agreed set of training modules for core and advanced fraud investigators – a first step towards common standards across the two groups of staff.**

Evaluation of attitudes

4.18 Current public attitudes on social security fraud have already been benchmarked, and the key results are set out in this chapter. The Government will repeat this research to inform our programme of culture change, and evaluate its impact.

Chapter Five

Developing security from beginning to end

Aim Two

To design and operate policies and systems which minimise fraud.

5.1 Our strategy of combating fraud is integral to the development of a modern service.

5.2 Welfare services are:

- **too often passive, with an emphasis on recording contributions and paying out money, rather than actively helping as many people as possible to move towards work and achieve independence;**
- **too complex and fragmented: we need services which employ modern methods so that they meet customers' needs and are easy to use; and**
- **insecure: in a modern service, we must ensure that we are paying money only to those who need it, so that we can afford to spend more on measures which promote prosperity such as training and education to assist people into work.**

5.3 The transformation of one of the largest and most complex systems in the country in order to achieve an Active Modern Service requires a disciplined and comprehensive approach. The system involves 90,000 staff in the Department of Social Security, 15,000 in local authorities, and 30,000 in the Employment Service operating from literally hundreds of sites and reliant on numerous and diverse computer systems. Building a modern service will not come about by an initiative here or there.

5.4 This breadth of approach and discipline is required particularly when tackling fraud and unintentional error. There are many ways in which fraud and error can creep into the social security system. We need to look across all our processes, from beginning to end, and systematically evaluate risks and identify counter-measures.

5.5 Some of the risks lie beyond immediate Department of Social Security responsibilities. For example, claims for Child Benefit rely significantly on the child's birth certificate, but the responsibility for the issue of these certificates lies outside the Department of Social Security. So we must look across organisational boundaries, working with other parts of central government, with local authorities and other public bodies, and with the private sector.

5.6 This chapter sets out the Government's strategy to minimise fraud and error, from the beginning to the end of our systems.

- **How we will prevent fraud and error through *benefit design* (Chapter 5.1).**
- **How we will prevent fraud and error through *individual account management* (Chapter 5.2).**
- **How we will detect and investigate suspicious cases – *detection* (Chapter 5.3).**
- **How we will recover overpayments, and sanction fraudulent behaviour – *enforcement* (Chapter 5.4).**
- **How we will give *assurance* that these initiatives are working and that the results are effectively *evaluated* (Chapter 5.5).**

■ 5.1 BENEFIT DESIGN

Prevention by design

5.1.1 The fight against fraud has evolved over time. First, there has to be recognition that there is a problem. In the United Kingdom, this has only happened at the political level recently. Once identified as a problem, the initial response was to find occurrences of fraud and stop them. This focus on detection can be driven by measurable activity and targets, and has so far been the mainstay of anti-fraud work in the social security system.

5.1.2 The prize, though, is to go a stage further and prevent fraud from occurring in the first place. This will save more, both in the cost of administering benefits (by cutting down on rework of claims and the cost of recovering benefits) and the costs of benefits themselves (since even the best detection systems cannot catch all fraud). It will also boost public confidence in the system.

5.1.3 The social security system is extremely complex. The rules governing Income Support, just one benefit, cover many pages of legislation. This creates an environment where those claiming benefits, and in some cases the staff administering the benefits, can easily be confused or make mistakes.

5.1.4 A distinction needs to be made between people who deliberately claim fraudulently and those who are confused by the benefit rules. The Government has a duty to ensure people are not caught out by the complexity of the system. That is why the Government has already taken steps towards introducing clearer rules, which are more readily understood and better communicated.

5.1.5 Before October 1997, benefit was paid on proof of need and not, for example, on proof of identity. But now all claims for Income Support require the claimant to produce all the necessary supporting evidence requested on the claim form before the claim is processed and benefit is paid. Further improvements are also planned.

- **The *1998 Social Security Act* contains measures to simplify and streamline decision-making and appeals in order to create a simpler and clearer system for customers and staff. In addition, changes to Social Fund loans should encourage customers to provide honest and accurate information.**
- **The structure of *National Insurance contributions* will be simplified from 1 April 1999 replacing four rates with a single rate for employers.**

5.1.6 The detailed rules governing benefit entitlement, and contribution conditions, may also encourage behaviour which is fraudulent. Much of the fraud identified in *Benefit Reviews* stems from claimants breaking one of three key rules:

- **the rule that reduces income-related benefits when earnings cross a low weekly threshold;**
- **the rule that means that two people declaring that they live together as a couple receive less benefit than two who pretend they live alone; and**
- **the rule that reduces income-related benefits where a person's financial capital exceeds £3,000.**

5.1.7 At a conservative estimate, fraud around these three rules amounts to £1.3 billion a year in Income Support/Jobseeker's Allowance and Invalid Care Allowance, rising to £1.7 billion if Housing Benefit is included.

5.1.8 The principles behind these rules are clear, but each involves a trade-off. The earnings rules are unchanged since their introduction in 1988: for example, the weekly amount which can be earned by a single person without loss of benefit is £5. This ensures that Jobseeker's Allowance is quickly reduced as earnings rise, but only if they are declared. Wherever the threshold is set, some individuals will not declare earnings. But a low threshold can also make the wider public tolerant of such behaviour, and undermine support for action against fraud.

- **The Government is *reviewing the benefit rules* which are most frequently broken, to see if the rules put an unfair burden on honesty. Here discussion will centre on whether the rules achieve the right balance between the cost to the taxpayer, the individual's natural wish to improve their own lot, the level of fraud, and the public's willingness to support action to police rules.**

5.1.9 More generally, all policy development needs to take account of the scope for improving the security and integrity of the social security system. There will always be competing objectives in developing policy, in particular between customer service issues, costs of administrative systems, and action to make benefit payments correct right from the start of a claim. Since new benefits are not designed and introduced very often, it is important to take the opportunity to ensure that, wherever possible, any changes in information technology or changes to benefit rules are accompanied by **raising the defences against fraud** of existing benefits. But concerns about security and integrity have taken too low a priority, reflecting the low awareness of fraud generally among politicians and policy makers.

- **The Government is now exploring what are called risk management techniques. This approach highlights the areas and actions most open to fraud. The results of these studies are being used to shape anti-fraud policies as well as the most effective deployment of staff.**

■ 5.2 INDIVIDUAL ACCOUNT MANAGEMENT

Prevention through the active management of new cases

5.2.1 Securing the gateways to the National Insurance system and to benefits is a critical step in preventing fraud and unintended error. A successful, but fraudulent, claim for Child Benefit could go on robbing the taxpayer for 19 years. A fraudster who successfully establishes a false identity could have a lifetime of opportunity to cheat the social security system, unless adequate checks are carried out routinely.

■ Example One

A woman stole nearly £60,000 by fraudulently continuing to claim a pension for her dead mother, a fraud which only came to light when enquiries were made ahead of a celebratory telegram for her mother's 100th 'birthday'.

■ Example Two

More than £42,000 was stolen by a woman who claimed Income Support, Housing Benefit and Council Tax Benefit for over three years but did not declare the earnings she received from her employment. The fraud was uncovered by an anti-fraud exercise run by the local authority in her area.

5.2.2 The Government has already taken several steps to tighten up gateways to the system:

- **The overriding importance of accuracy has been demonstrated by the Government setting the Benefits Agency only a *target for accuracy* in 1998/99, formally dropping the previous (and competing) target for the speed with which new claims were cleared.**
- **There were almost 1.8 million activities to *check new claims* in 1997/98 (an increase of 63 per cent over the last year of the previous Government), including visits to claimants' homes, office interviews and contacts by telephone. Around 2 million checks on new claims are planned for 1998/99, an investment of £46.8 million with expected savings of £733 million.**

- Since October 1997, prior to payment, all claims to Income Support require customers to confirm their identity as well as their need for the benefit (Section 19 of the Fraud Act). In parallel, as a result of the Benefits Agency Evidence Project, Benefits Agency staff have been using a *thorough and detailed approach to handling new claims for Income Support*, which ensures that all relevant evidence is gathered, checked and thoroughly evaluated before any money is paid out.
- The Department of Social Security has begun to establish a *single database* to hold individual's personal details (name, address, age, National Insurance number, etc) in a common format. This will replace the current, often inconsistent, data held on each separate benefit system. So far this new database, the Personal Details Computer System is in use for Child Benefit and for most Income Support claims. By October 1998 it will be in use for all Income Support claims, and also for changes of circumstances.
- From April 1998, a prototype involving Lewisham Borough Council has implemented a daily electronic *transfer of Income Support and Jobseeker's Allowance data* from the Benefits Agency to the Council, to replace the previous daily paper-based process. The data enables the Council to make more accurate determinations of claims to Housing Benefit by using this data. This should enable the Council to speed up the processing of Housing Benefit claims and help reduce overpayments of Housing Benefit.
- Since April 1998, a prototype new service has been established in two parts of the country, enabling *lone parents to make claims for Income Support, Housing Benefit and Council Tax Benefit through a single process.* Instead of dealing separately with the Benefits Agency and their local authority (and the Child Support Agency for maintenance), a single set of details is taken and verified once, with clear advantages for security and integrity in terms of consistency of information.
- Closer Working Project arrangements between the Benefits Agency and the Child Support Agency have increased the proportion of lone parents pursuing maintenance from absent parents, reducing the extent of incorrect or fraudulent payments. Estimates from the evaluation of this work indicate that the proportion of new claimants who co-operate with the Child Support Agency has increased from just under half to around three-quarters. Previously almost half of all application forms returned involved claiming 'good cause' for not co-operating with the Child Support Agency. Under closer working, genuine 'good cause' is identified sooner and dealt with quickly, offering a better service to the customer. Further phases of closer working initiatives between the two agencies are already planned.

- **The Contributions Agency has further developed a comprehensive logging system which ensures that all applications for National Insurance numbers can be accounted for and tracked through the system. The statistical information available from the system will be used to identify trends and will be used in future risk profiling initiatives.**

5.2.3 The Government will build on this initial platform over the rest of the Parliament. The priorities will be determined from a continuing learning process, identifying the risks and weaknesses in the management of new claims, and targeting investment where it will be most effective. Plans for the future already include:

- **improving business processes and the way claims are handled, using formal risk management techniques to establish what mistakes staff make in managing ongoing claims, and to devise ways to make it less likely that errors will be made. This new, more secure approach will be rolled out first in Income Support from April 1999;**

- **safeguarding the *gateways* to *National Insurance numbers.* The Government is strengthening the security on each of the three main entrances to the National Insurance system. These involve the conversion of Child Benefit numbers into a National Insurance number, the awarding of National Insurance numbers to people who, after coming to this country, have a right to claim social security benefits and lastly, issuing National Insurance numbers to those arriving in this country and presenting themselves for work. It is continuing a process of combing through the stock of National Insurance numbers to take out those which are bogus (there are well documented weaknesses in the way that the previous administration issued National Insurance numbers), and, in order to prevent fraud involving staff, it is strengthening the vetting procedures in relation to key staff involved in issuing National Insurance numbers;**

- **spreading the best practice to safeguard access to Housing Benefit. The introduction of what is called the *Verification Framework,* developed in consultation with local authorities, provides guidance on the processes to be followed to deliver Housing Benefit and Council Tax Benefit securely. The framework is a voluntary code, which some 100 local authorities have already decided to implement. Local authorities have been invited to apply for extra funding this year – £15 million has been made available – to help them implement the Framework;**

- **roll out of the *Personal Details Computer System* to all benefits administered by the Benefits Agency. For the first time, this will give staff a single, consistent database of personal details – against**

which to check any new claims – rather than the present, often inconsistent data held on several systems. Income Support is being taken on in 1998, followed in 1999 by Jobseeker's Allowance, Retirement and Widow's Pension, Incapacity Benefit and short-term benefits. By the end of 2000, all benefits will use this system. All this will improve service to claimants while at the same time securing taxpayers' money much more effectively; and

- **local authority staff administering Housing Benefit/Council Tax Benefit will be provided with on-line access to contemporary Benefits Agency data on Income Support and Jobseeker's Allowance. This will enable local authorities to check current details held by the Benefits Agency against those claiming Housing Benefit/Council Tax Benefit.**

Prevention through the management of continuing cases

5.2.4 In addition to preventing fraud by securing the gateways to the social security system, we must also prevent fraud and error creeping in once benefit is in payment, or a National Insurance account established. From the results of the *Benefit Reviews* we believe that in some 70 per cent of cases, benefit fraud and error began **after** the initial claim.

5.2.5 Here we need the active support of voters. In countering fraud it will help the Government if individuals pay careful attention to when they should report changes in their circumstances. Our Active Modern Service aims to make such reporting easier. The more individuals help in this way, the more staff will be able to concentrate their attention on tracking down serious abuses.

5.2.6 The Government has already taken action to improve the security and integrity of claims once they are in the system. The measures implemented so far are shown in the box below.

- **In 1996/97, 1.19 million claims were subject to targeted reviews in order to check continued entitlement. During 1997/98, this figure rose to 1.61 million cases (an increase of 35 per cent). All these reviews involve direct contact with claimants often by unannounced home visits. In 1997/98 reviews generated £212 million in savings. The number of targeted reviews planned for 1998/99 has increased by 700,000, to 2.2 million, with almost all this increase focused on home visits.**

- **An *extension of data matching* across different benefit computer systems, which identifies cases to investigate (for example, where earnings are declared on one system but not another, or where two claimants are making separate claims for the same children). In 1997/98 the service in the Benefits Agency generated some 137,000 referrals resulting in reported savings of £84 million.**

- **The introduction of a new data-matching service for local authorities which matches Housing Benefit/Council Tax Benefit data against that held by other local authorities and with Benefits Agency data on a quarterly basis. The service is still rolling out, with over 200 local authorities live so far. This service for local authorities has generated over 30,000 referrals to date, with over £5 million in savings.**

- **Introduction of a month-on-month programme of Area *Benefit Reviews* which are surveys of Income Support and Jobseeker's Allowance claims carried out in all 13 geographical areas of the Benefits Agency. By sampling the stock of cases in this way we get a rolling picture of fraud and incorrectness (see Chapter Six). This in turn improves our knowledge about how to target effort to keep information up to date.**

5.2.7 At present targeted reviews form the major part of work to keep claims correct. But we can do more to support this work. The Government is:

- **tightening gateways, while placing the major emphasis on the accuracy of the claim. Modernising the way we ensure integrity is a very substantial challenge. The first step will be the introduction of a revised process for Income Support in April 1999;**

- **publishing a code of practice for data-matching this autumn. The commitment to do so was made during the passage of the Fraud Act 1997, which gave new powers to the Department of Social Security to accept data from Inland Revenue, Customs and Excise, and agencies of the Home Office. This will be published by October 1998;**

- **extending data-matching to include information held by Inland Revenue, Customs and Excise, and agencies of the Home Office. We have begun to develop the mechanisms for this work which will be initiated during next year; and**

- **reviewing the existing data protection legislation, to identify further possibilities for harnessing data sources beyond the Department of Social Security.**

■ 5.3 DETECTION

Detection and investigation of suspicious cases

5.3.1 The previous section set out the Government's plans for improving the prevention of fraud throughout the social security system. Unfortunately, it is inevitable that some fraud will enter even the best run systems. Our approach to tackling fraud from the beginning to the end of our systems must therefore cover the detection and investigation of suspicious cases.

5.3.2 Traditionally, this is the area in which successive Governments have invested: fraud investigators have been on the streets for many years undertaking surveillance and interviews under caution, using a wide range of techniques. While we increase our effort in prevention, we must also maintain the ability to police the benefit systems. The 5,000 'bobbies on the beat' in Benefits Agency benefit fraud investigation received one-and-a-half million referrals in 1997/98 from the public, other members of staff, the National Benefit Fraud Hotline, other agencies, police, local authorities, the Immigration Service, data-matching, etc. Since July 1997, 305 of the 1,700 fraud staff employed by local authorities (1,100 directly on investigations) have been appointed as inspectors with new powers, under the 1997 Fraud Act, to enter business premises and examine records.

5.3.3 Our welfare system, which is rightly accessible to citizens, is also open to serious organised criminal gangs. As fraudsters become more sophisticated, we need to be able to respond.

5.3.4 The Department of Social Security already has a force of around 300 specially trained officers to undertake investigation into serious fraud. In London, the local authorities have the London Organised Fraud Investigation Team, tackling Housing Benefit fraud across boroughs in the capital. These staff work alongside police, Customs and Excise, Inland Revenue and Immigration officers and carry out intelligence gathering and surveillance, in order to disrupt and destroy gangs engaged in theft through fraudulent claims, counterfeit GIROs, theft of mail bags, etc. Department of Social Security and local authority staff work together at an operational level on many investigations, and are always looking to improve experience and expertise.

5.3.5 Recent achievements in this area are in the box below.

- **In 1997/98 the Benefits Agency carried out 549,000 successful *investigations on individuals or gangs* leading to benefit being stopped and this led to 12,000 prosecutions with savings of £705.5 million.**
- **Of the 549,000 investigations, 1,742 were complicated investigations into organised fraud by the Benefits Agency Security Investigation Service, which resulted in 626 prosecutions, with a 92 per cent success rate in conviction.**

5.3.6 Serious fraud is a particular threat, and we need to design appropriate counter-measures. During the next year, the Government is intent on:

- **considering investment in a *national intelligence system* to counter serious fraud;**
- ***cross agency working on enforcement,* building on small-scale links already in place. To do this we will need to invest in better management information systems to record and track all the thousands of activities across not only the Department of Social Security and local authorities, but beyond (where cases involve police, Home Office, etc);**
- ***extending the security of benefit order-books and GIRO cheques,* for example introducing bar-code scanners more widely across the country, and reviewing the rules governing replacement of 'lost' GIRO cheques;**
- ***working with local authorities in combating Housing Benefit and Council Tax Benefit fraud* by a series of measures including the Housing Benefit Matching Service and using new powers under the Fraud Act, including prevention of redirection of local authority benefit post and the appointment of inspectors with powers of entry; and**
- **the Government will *take new steps to tackle landlord fraud,* where a single fraudulent landlord can obtain thousands of pounds a week in public funds. A number of steps will be considered, including:**
  - **work to measure thoroughly the extent of this type of fraud;**
  - **in the light of evaluation of a current pilot exercise in London, the creation of specialist teams in other regions to counter landlord fraud;**
  - **the establishing of a register for landlords who wish to receive public funds; and**
  - **working to ensure that all landlords in receipt of public funds pay the tax that is due.**

5.4 ENFORCEMENT

Sanctions and recovery

5.4.1 Too many social security fraudsters escape effective punishment. Last year, the Benefits Agency prosecuted 12,000 fraudsters, but many more went unpunished and over a third of those taken to Magistrates' Court received only a conditional discharge.

5.4.2 While Government agencies are encouraged to recover overpayments, and last year the Benefits Agency collected on 900,000 overpayments, worth some £120 million, there continue to be much larger sums not recovered. There is also a comparable problem for local authorities in recovering Housing Benefit and Council Tax Benefit wrongly paid.

5.4.3 This state of affairs will not continue. It would not make sense to prosecute every offence (since the cost of some prosecutions will exceed the sums at stake), but it does make sense to prosecute some small-scale fraud so that all fraudsters face the risk of prosecution. The Government has already made enforcement a more credible deterrent by:

- **introducing administrative penalties: where a fraudster can expect a court sentence, these penalties (the amount of the overpayment plus 30 per cent on top) offer swifter and more cost-effective sanctions;**
- **introducing the authority for Department of Social Security officials to issue formal cautions, where a fraudster confesses, which will form part of the fraudster's criminal record and may be taken into account in any subsequent court case; and**
- **announcing its intention to prosecute some frauds irrespective of size, to remove any ability to steal a 'safe' amount.**

5.4.4 However, there is some confusion about when to use which sanction, and little consistency of application across the country. For various reasons (including weaknesses in incentive arrangements) some local authorities have not prosecuted offenders at all. Court sentencing policy is not always consistently applied. This is out of step with the seriousness with which we regard benefit crime.

The Government will:

- **begin to develop this year a *national framework for the use of sanctions* by all agencies involved in social security administration, to promote consistent treatment that commands public support;**
- ***review the approach of all agencies* involved in prosecuting and case handling for benefit fraud offenders;**
- ***monitor the use made of the new sanctions now available,* to learn lessons about how they are used and viewed by the public and staff; and**
- **increase and *integrate debt recovery action across Government,* to prevent offenders avoiding repayment of fraudulently obtained public funds.**

■ 5.5 EVALUATION AND ASSURANCE

Assurance

5.5.1 In carrying out this massive programme of change and improvement in end-to-end security, we need to know whether what we are doing is working and whether it is leading to:

- **improvements in performance;**
- **integrity of systems;**
- **maintenance of service to customers; and**
- **meeting our strategic aims.**

5.5.2 There are already several mechanisms which provide elements of limited assurance:

- **the Benefits Agency pursue compliance through a number of measures including specialist teams who validate accuracy of claims and of Weekly Benefit Savings at local, area and national level. There is also a high profile compliance group, led by a Director of Field Operations;**
- **the Contributions Agency use a number of measures including Director's Assurance Teams; and**
- **in local authorities, the Audit Commission operates to ensure that controls are in place.**

5.5.3 The most significant new development in this area has been the Government's creation of the Benefit Fraud Inspectorate. Launched in November 1997, these experts plan to inspect the benefit administration of each local authority, and each Department of Social Security agency, over a five to six year period. The Benefit Fraud Inspectorate will be making reports on their inspections, which will be published. The detailed inspections, by specially trained, experienced staff, are already providing specific recommendations to improve performance for the bodies inspected. Information from Benefit Fraud Inspectorate inspections will also help drive up standards of performance elsewhere, and provide a contribution to policy development. The box opposite summarises the results from the first inspection earlier this year in Blackpool.

Blackpool Borough Council was the first formal inspection by the Benefit Fraud Inspectorate. The 84-page, detailed report makes eight major recommendations to address the findings of the inspection by:

- **securing improvements to the claim form and verification processes;**
- **improving the number of payments made correctly first time;**
- **enhancing internal controls (for example, by securing the information technology system);**
- **controlling and reducing the level of outstanding overpayments;**
- **increasing the emphasis in anti-fraud work on landlords;**
- **making fraud investigation work better targeted and more rigorous;**
- **improving working practices with the Benefits Agency and the Employment Service; and**
- **improving internal guidance to fraud investigators on claiming Weekly Benefit Savings.**

Chapter Six

Environment

Aim Three

To create an environment in which the work against fraud can flourish.

6.1 By taking a holistic approach to policy and the design and operation of systems (Chapter Five), the Government is making progress against fraud. The extent of that progress also depends on improvements elsewhere, in particular in:

- **our ability to *measure* the nature and extent of fraud, identify weaknesses in the system, and to measure the success of activities to reduce fraud;**
- **the way in which we go about *funding* benefit administration, in particular the financial incentives within Government to act against fraud; and**
- **the degree of *co-operation* across different agencies, the local authorities, the rest of Government and into the private sector.**

6.2 These issues effectively determine an environment within which activity against fraud takes place. The challenge is to ensure that the environment supports that work, rather than hindering it.

6.3 The present environment clearly reflects a world in which fraud was a new item on the political agenda, where the imperative was to kick start action within a system that ignored fraud. So, armed only with a simple measure of successful detection of fraud, the previous Government built a funding system which promoted reactive, detective anti-fraud work.

6.4 This approach stimulated action. But it is increasingly clear that it also created a number of problems:

- ***funding for one year at a time* hinders planning and staff development; and with savings required in each year, no account is taken of benefits which might flow in subsequent years;**
- ***the Benefits Agency and local authority staff find themselves in competition* to detect fraud and record savings, rather than co-operating with each other;**

- *rewarding administrative systems which let in fraud* – **which can then be found – rather than incentivising investment in systems which prevent fraud in the first place is a perverse way of going about stamping out fraud. With local authority funding linked directly to the level of fraud found, there is evidence from the National Audit Office, the Audit Commission and the Benefit Fraud Inspectorate that some local authorities** *overstate their achievements*; **overstatement has also occurred within the Benefits Agency; and**
- *a concentration on operational efficiency* **with less concern for the overall efficiency of operational resources in controlling benefit spend.**

6.5 This Government's approach has moved on. We are designing and operating systems, in particular measurement and funding, which:

- **promote co-operation of all parties in the fight against fraud;**
- **promote prevention, to stop fraud occurring in the first place, while retaining a capability to detect and investigate it;**
- **reward good practice; and**
- **ensure effective decision-making on resource allocation.**

6.6 Our programme of action is set out below, and must be continually informed by the experience of front-line staff.

Measurement

6.7 Accurate measurement of fraud and incorrectness is critical because:

- **it is the ultimate benchmark against which to measure** ***the success of our fraud strategy;*** **and**
- **information about the nature and extent of fraud, based on robust statistical methodologies, is a critical platform for** ***assessing and managing risks.***

6.8 The previous Government established the programme of national *Benefit Reviews,* looking at individual benefits in turn, beginning in 1994 with Income Support (see Chapter Two). These are national reviews, and so there are no estimates of fraud in individual geographical areas which can inform local management action. And with only two benefits so far reviewed twice, there is no consistent series of results over time.

6.9 The Government is already developing prototypes of new reviews, to generate both local and continuing estimates of the nature and extent of fraud:

- **each of the 13 Benefits Agency Areas is now measuring fraud and incorrectness on Income Support and Jobseeker's Allowance each month; and**
- **nine volunteer local authorities have signed up to an experimental programme of reviews of Housing Benefit in the areas covered by the local authority, with the results of the first reviews due in October 1998, and two more in the next two years.**

6.10 We have also broadened the measurement effort, by investing in a series of initiatives to improve both our understanding of fraud, and of what actions work against fraud:

- **33 local authorities have volunteered to test other ways to measure success in countering fraud through prevention and deterrence, with work starting later this year; and**
- **the Benefits Agency has developed, and is trialling at several sites, 26 new performance indicators and 11 alternative measures to supplement the existing measures of activity (some evaluation of this work is due in October 1998 and a clearer picture is likely to emerge in the first half of 1999).**

6.11 All this work is building towards a comprehensive Performance Measurement Framework. This will provide:

- **a *measure of outcome,* which is the level of programme loss broken down by cause, for example fraud or customer error. This goes beyond the measures already in place and those being trialled, with the aim to bring together, consistently and with confidence about accuracy, all the available information in the system on the level and nature of fraud and incorrectness. Such systems are used extensively in the private sector, particularly in the financial sector, for a range of purposes from measuring the level of credit card fraud to sizing the risks attached to insurance claims. The measure might be designed and operated as a public private partnership.**
- **a *measure of capability* of the Department of Social Security and local authorities to minimise programme loss – this would be a new development, bringing in techniques used in the private sector and in some other parts of the public sector – the aim is to construct a framework within which to identify weaknesses and assess priorities for action.**
- **a *measure of activity* to establish, resource and target the range of activities to reduce programme loss.**

6.12 The viability of this approach, in particular the costs and timescales, depend critically on the assessment of the various prototypes already underway.

Funding and incentives

6.13 The Government spent some £3 billion last year on benefit administration: £2.5 billion on the Benefits Agency, and £0.4 billion on local authorities for their work administering benefits.

6.14 Within this total there are several ring-fenced elements which may be spent only on activity related to security. Last year, the Benefits Agency received £361 million for fraud and security work (15 per cent of its total funding) while local authorities received £90 million (23 per cent of their funding for benefit administration). This ring-fenced funding is provided on the basis that the Benefits Agency and local authorities then save much larger amounts of programme expenditure by finding and stopping fraud. This year, for example, the Benefits Agency target was £2.1 billion and the local authorities target was just over £0.4 billion.

6.15 Over the last three years, the incentive funding has grown sharply as has the amount of fraud detected. For example, fraud savings by local authorities, grew from £224 million in 1995/96 to £371 million in 1997/98, earning the local authorities additional subsidy rising to £65 million in 1997/98. The regime clearly has an effect on performance against fraud, and illustrates sharply how funding rules influence behaviour.

6.16 If the overall strategy against fraud and incorrectness is to move **away from detection towards prevention,** there must be **parallel moves in the funding regime.** The work on measurement outlined above is clearly critical. But in parallel with this, the Government, working with local authorities, will review the funding arrangements to ensure that they provide the best possible support for action against fraud while also encouraging efficiency and cost-effectiveness.

Fostering co-operation

6.17 Fraud is not something that any one agency can successfully tackle by acting alone. The security issues raised by fraud cross organisational boundaries. It is critical that environment for tackling fraud promotes co-operation, within central Government, with local authorities, and into the private sector. The plans to review funding seek to reduce one element of competition, between the Benefits Agency and local authorities. But there is more that can be done in this field.

6.18 First, we must develop our strategy in a way which is **inclusive** involving all the stakeholders in design and in implementation, both practitioners and policy makers. **Specialist knowledge** must be used in tackling this complex problem. The strategy set out in this Green Paper has already benefited from this approach, drawing on the experience and views of representatives from a wide variety of backgrounds, from both Government consultation of interested parties in both public and private sectors, and more detailed work by Department of Social Security and local authority officials. We will continue to welcome the views of experts in the field.

6.19 In two particular areas, it will be especially important to maximise co-operation and apply specialist knowledge. The Government:

- **will ensure a systematic and proactive review of the civil and criminal law and the extent to which it helps or hinders work to tackle fraud, taking full account of the direct experience of anti-fraud officers; and**
- **will also monitor the latest information technology developments in order to ensure that information technology is used as effectively as possible to counter fraud.**

6.20 In order to drive forward co-operation across government, a Ministerial group will be established covering those Departments whose processes have a bearing on the integrity of the social security system. This group would have three immediate objectives:

- **to organise co-operation across central government;**
- **to consider ways to draw local authorities and the private sector into the process of co-operation; and**
- **as a first specific task, to assess the merits of having officers accountable for fraud issues in each of the participating Departments (the Government has already begun this process by the recent appointments of Directors of Fraud Strategy at senior civil service level in the Department of Social Security and in the Department of Health).**

Other key elements of the Government's approach

6 21 As well as operating an inclusive approach to the development and implementation of the strategy against fraud, the Government is also committed to operate in a way which is:

- ***comprehensive,* tackling all areas with all relevant methods – internal and external fraud, employer and claimant fraud, landlord and tenant fraud;**
- ***balanced,* covering low-value but high-volume fraud, medium and high value sophisticated and complex fraud;**
- ***fair,* applying principles of good practice, with high standards of objectivity; and**
- ***effective,* with demonstrable reductions in the amount of insecure programme spending.**

Chapter Seven

Professionalism

Aim Four

To develop a highly-skilled anti-fraud profession.

7.1 Until quite recently, public service was built on an assumption of respect from customers. Public service relied on the honesty of its customers. That trust, sadly can no longer be relied upon. While most claimants are honest, too many people do abuse the system, some on a huge scale. The perception of public services free from fraud and abuse needs radical revision.

7.2 Fraud and abuse occur not only from individuals working the system, but more recently, from organised gang fraud. No government will ever know the full extent of fraud. But, as with freedom, security requires eternal vigilance, and the Government's fight against fraud must build up the expertise and confidence of its anti-fraud staff.

The current position

7.3 Some public sector areas have in the past left staff engaged in tackling fraud to develop their skills on their own initiative. This has led to varying levels of expertise in different areas. **Our aim must be to overcome these differences and for the very best of today's practices to become the common practices of tomorrow.**

7.4 A profession can operate as the collective memory of those working in a particular area. To date, there has been no conscious, co-ordinated effort to introduce professionalism to anti-fraud work, so that all too often the wheel has been reinvented in different organisations, and in different parts of the country within the same organisations.

7.5 The proposals below illustrate how the Government values those who undertake difficult, complex and sometimes dangerous work in protecting taxpayers' money; and how the resource they represent can be developed and focused to best effect.

Proposals

7.6 We must develop a body of highly-skilled anti-fraud specialists capable of tackling fraud in the same way other professions have applied their skills, with:

- **common skill standards;**
- **common core training for all staff involved in anti-fraud work;**
- **training accreditation;**
- **continuous learning and development;**
- **common principles of good practice; and**
- **a common approach across central and local government, the public and areas such as the Post Office and the private sector.**

7.7 **Common core training is essential,** ensuring staff have the required skills. This starts at a practical skills-based **Foundation Level**, progressing to a more strategic **Advanced Level**. It should both raise the skills levels of all staff and ensure all anti-fraud officers can work co-operatively, using common methods in a common and universally understood framework. Refresher courses should maintain high levels of skill and performance.

7.8 **Training must be assessed,** and those who successfully complete it will be independently accredited with **an appropriate professional qualification.** Accreditation will help set and maintain standards of excellence in this area of work.

7.9 **Training should be structured so as to ensure continuous development,** with staff moving through each level and, if they wish, on to appropriate academic qualifications. In this way the valuable resource that such staff represent can be nurtured and retained for the public benefit.

7.10 There should be **clear principles of good practice** outlining how anti-fraud officers should tackle fraud. They will prioritise **fairness, objectivity, professionalism, expertise, propriety and foresight.** They will seek to ensure that all anti-fraud work correctly identifies the guilty parties, while protecting the innocent from abuse, and minimising losses to public funds.

7.11 Based on these principles should be a **comprehensive code of conduct** for anti-fraud staff, and a **code of good investigative practice**. Drawing on the widest range of good practice, these codes will further regulate methods of countering fraud and help ensure that the highest standards are applied and maintained.

7.12 Anti-fraud work needs to be managed in the context of parallel projects to reform the social security system, which seek not only to protect its resources from misappropriation, but to ensure top quality, cost effective delivery of services to the public. To further strengthen this management process, proposals will be developed for **a security management framework for anti-fraud managers**. This framework will reflect the wide scope of this paper, ensuring that managers apply a comprehensive and consistent approach to the problem.

7.13 The result of developing and applying these initiatives will be a body of highly-skilled anti-fraud officers working within a professional framework to the highest standards of performance and integrity. A final step will then be to develop a system for providing a further focus for standards, to assist in the regulation of practice, to sponsor training and research and to ensure expertise is applied swiftly and directly to anti-fraud work. The Government will urgently consider how such centres of excellence can quickly be established.

Conclusion

7.14 This Chapter has described key measures which are being developed to bring professionalism to bear in protecting the social security system. While many of the measures can be applied relatively quickly, producing appropriate benefits, their positive effects are best viewed in the long term where a real investment in skills and expertise will reap dividends.

7.15 Ultimately, the larger the body of tested expertise in anti-fraud work, the better the contribution to policy development and implementation, and the more effective the Government's work, to ensure that public funds finance better systems and services rather than being lost to fraud.

Chapter Eight

Timetable for action

8.1 This Green Paper is the Government's first audit for the nation on its strategy for countering fraud in social security. Each year the Government will present to Parliament, and thereby the country, an annual anti-fraud audit.

8.2 This section illustrates how the various elements of the strategy are being taken forward, identifying:

- **action already underway;**
- **action in the rest of 1998/99; and**
- **action next year and beyond.**

8.3 All this is in addition to the many initiatives or developments which the Government has already put in place in its first year in office, recorded in particular in Chapters Five and Six.

Action already underway

8.4 The Government is:

- **redesigning the way claims for Income Support are processed, to prevent fraudsters gaining benefit in the first place;**
- **setting up a new Ministerial group to oversee anti-fraud strategy across central government, and to lead co-operation in the fight against fraud with local authorities, other public sector bodies and the private sector;**
- **developing methods for cross-checking records within the National Insurance Recording System, as the first step towards cleaning up bogus National Insurance numbers;**
- **strengthening the defence of the three gateways into the National Insurance system;**
- **toughening up recruitment practices to limit the opportunities for internal fraud within the National Insurance Fund;**

- **running and evaluating a prototype modern service in Lewisham, which involves daily electronic transfer of Income Support and Jobseeker's Allowance data from the Benefits Agency to Lewisham Borough Council, in order to make Housing Benefit administration more secure and more efficient;**
- **completing a code of practice on the use of data and data-matching to identify possible fraud - this is a necessary preliminary to extending data-matching with Inland Revenue and Customs and Excise. The code will be published this autumn;**
- **reviewing the targeting of anti-fraud investigation;**
- **implementing its policy to prosecute even some very low value frauds, removing 'no-go' areas where a fraudster can otherwise assume that he or she will avoid prosecution;**
- **pursuing more prosecutions under the Theft Act, rather than the Social Security Administration Act;**
- **implementing across the board the first year's programme of inspections by the Benefit Fraud Inspectorate;**
- **testing prototypes in the Benefits Agency and local authorities of new measures of fraud and performance against fraud; and**
- **agreeing common core skills and professional training for fraud investigators in Department of Social Security agencies and local authorities;**

Action in the rest of 1998/99

8.5 The Government will be:

- **implementing across the country the redesigned, more secure, process for managing claims for Income Support;**
- **funding the first local authorities to implement the *Verification Framework*, which raises the defence against Housing Benefit fraud;**
- **setting up a trial of data-matching with Inland Revenue;**
- **installing computer terminals in all local authorities that request them, to give access to benefit claims data held by the Benefits Agency;**
- **extending the use of barcodes as a means of preventing GIRO cheque and order book fraud;**
- **reviewing the incentives for funding security work to improve prevention, as well as detection, and to promote co-operation between the Benefits Agency and local authorities;**

- **reporting on the extent and nature of identity fraud;**
- **establishing and implementing a national framework of a broad and flexible range of sanctions to enhance those already available;**
- **gaining greater staff co-operation by promoting their awareness of ways in which the system is attacked, while simultaneously improving their compliance on operating procedures;**
- **gaining greater public support in the fight against all fraudsters, and winning public support for the principle of demonstrating entitlement to benefit; and**
- **implementing for fraud investigators the agreed principles of good practice, common core training and continuous learning and development.**

Action next year and beyond

8.6 In the future, we will also:

- **establish the most effective way of handling the investigation of organised fraud against the social security system;**
- **building on the experience of completing earlier changes to Income Support, develop and implement more secure processes for managing claims to other major benefits;**
- **establish a criminal intelligence database for fraud investigation in the Benefits Agency and local authorities;**
- **review other entitlement rules to establish the right balance between the costs of administering the benefit, the level of fraud, and public support in tackling fraud;**
- **research further the extent and nature of landlord fraud; and**
- **build on current prototypes of new measurement systems to develop a comprehensive and consistent approach to measuring fraud and the performance measurement of activities to reduce fraud.**

Chapter Nine

2020 new vision

9.1 By 2020 our social security system will:

- **have been rebuilt with security as an integral part of the delivery of benefits from the outset of every claim, with all of the Department of Social Security's information technology systems reflecting this priority;**
- **be an active service responding effectively to individual needs and using well targeted checks and controls to deter fraud; and**
- **have staff clear about their role in delivering an Active Modern Service whereby:**
  - **the right payment is made to the right person, at the right time;**
  - **those eligible for claiming benefits are sought out and told of their entitlement; and**
  - **equal weight is given to countering fraud.**

9.2 We will also see:

- **a public which has a clearer view of the range of frauds being operated against the social security system, and which actively supports an effective anti-fraud strategy; and**
- **a professional and dedicated staff spearheading anti-fraud services, ever mindful of the need to stay ahead of the game as patterns of fraud and attacks by fraudsters change.**

9.3 We will have in place a whole series of checks across all aspects of benefits which will have reduced the level of social security fraud, and then maintained it at an irreducible minimum.

Annex

Benefit Reviews

To tackle social security fraud effectively, it is essential to establish a measure of the level of fraud. Starting as recently as 1994, the Department of Social Security has run a series of reviews of fraud and incorrectness in individual benefits - the *Benefit Reviews* - to try and determine the scale and nature of benefit fraud. These case examinations, involving access to internal and publicly available data, are followed by highly-structured interviews to establish the correctness of sampled claims. Beginning with Income Support and continuing with eight other benefits (three of these only to pilot stage, so far) these reviews have so far covered some 84 per cent of annual spend.

To understand the results of the Reviews, it is important to be quite clear about what we mean by fraud. In this Green Paper, estimates are presented for:

- **fraud (based on investigations where there is *evidence*, from the customer or a third party, that the circumstances do not match those on which the claim was paid; where the *benefit is then adjusted*; and an *intention to misrepresent* is assessed by Department of Social Security staff: investigating officers provide evidence only, and take no part in the assessment)[1];**
- **high suspicion of fraud (characterised by a balance of probability that fraud exists; in a majority of cases, payments are adjusted or stopped);**
- **low suspicion (where the balance of probabilities test is not met, nor is there usually enough evidence for a claim to be adjusted);**
- **incorrectness (where there is evidence of either customer or administrative error, and a claim is adjusted, but there is no suspicion of intentional misrepresentation); and**
- **correctness (or strictly, absence of any indicator to the contrary).**

The principal findings of the *Benefit Reviews* completed so far are shown in the table overleaf. Reflecting the conventions when they were publicised, the results combine estimates of fraud and high suspicion of fraud. Estimating fraud in Disability Living Allowance presents particular difficulties because entitlement depends on care and mobility needs which are not easily estimated other than through the formal adjudication process. As a result the estimates in the table for Disability Living Allowance will include errors by customers. The chart which follows the table presents figures for fraud, without estimates of suspected fraud.

[1]The Housing Benefit estimates are on a different basis.

Benefit Review	Date results published	Percentage of claims where fraud confirmed or strongly suspected	Total programme loss £m (estimated)
Income Support First review	July 1995	9.7%	1,409
Unemployment Benefit	July 1995	7.8%	86
Housing Benefit First review	January 1996	8%	905
Retirement Pension	March 1996	up to 0.13%	up to 40
Invalid Care Allowance	July 1996	6.5%	37
Disability Living Allowance	February 1997	12.2%	499
Income Support Second review	July 1997	11.1%	1,774
Housing Benefit Second review	due summer 1998		

Note: *Benefit Reviews* are sample excercises and all estimates are subject to statistical uncertainties.

Main types of fraud in income-related benefits

Income Support + income-based Jobseeker's Allowance + Housing Benefit

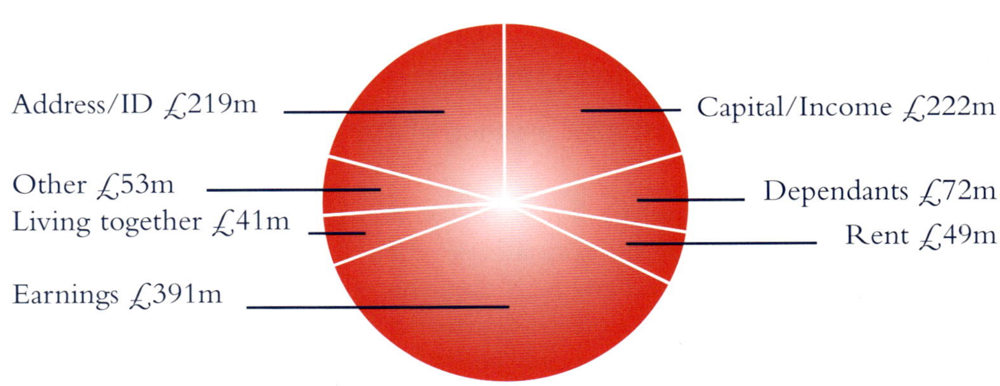

IS + JSA (IB) + HB: £1bn

Printed in the UK for The Stationery Office Limited
on behalf of the Controller of Her Majesty's Stationery Office
Dd 5068143 7/98 61743 Job No. J0053681